YOU MAKE IT WORK

TELEVISION

Authors: George and Shirley Coulter

Rourke Publications, Inc.
Vero Beach, Florida 32964

About the Authors

Award-winning teachers in the state of Wisconsin,
George and Shirley Coulter have now retired, but
remain active in the field of science education,
designing and presenting teacher workshops. Both
are published authors of books and articles in
national, professional journals in the field of science
education.

A book by Market Square Communications Incorporated
Pamela J.P. Schroeder, Editor
Sandra J. Shekels, Illustrator

Acknowledgements

Thanks to Cedar Creek Factory Stores and WAOW
TV 9 for providing the storyboard that appears on
page 21. Also, thanks to WAOW TV 9, Wausau, WI,
for their assistance in arranging photo locations.

Library of Congress Cataloging-in-Publication Data

Coulter, George, 1934-
    Television / by George and Shirley Coulter.
       p. cm. — (You make it work)
    Includes index.
    Summary: A look at the science that makes the picture tube work,
a view inside a TV studio, and a discussion of how television signals are
sent to homes everywhere.
    ISBN 0-86625-583-4
    1. Television—Juvenile literature. [1. Television.] I. Coulter,
Shirley, 1936-   . II. Title. III. Series.
TK6640.C68 1996
621.388—dc20   95-51374
                                        CIP
                                        AC

Printed in the U.S.A.

Illustrations are simplified examples meant to show general concepts rather than specific
technical detail.

TABLE OF CONTENTS

CHAPTER ONE

PLUG INTO TELEVISION

In at least one room of almost every home sits an amazing device. It's a device so interesting that most people stop and look at it almost every day. It's a television!

Just think what you can do with your television. You can transport yourself around the world with one fingertip! You can watch the Olympic Games wherever they're competing—in Japan, Germany or in the United States—right when it's happening.

A news flash breaks in to tell you about a storm that's coming your way. Your favorite TV show starts and you can sit back and laugh right along with the studio audience—live from New York!

Television is a powerful tool. It gives us ideas, information—and plenty of entertainment. Remember that it's your fingers at the controls. You and your family decide what to watch, how much to watch, and what to think of what you watch.

Without you, television is just a box full of wires and gadgets. Let's see how you make television work for you.

Television can take you anywhere in your neighborhood, or into outer space. Watching a game, you see the announcer and the action at the same time on a split screen. Then the action switches to an aerial shot from a blimp. Finally, it moves into an instant replay of the last score.

TV Takes Over

In 1946 there were 6,000 television sets in the United States. In the late 1990s that number grew to 145 million sets. There are at least two television sets in over 98 percent of our homes. They're turned on for an average of seven hours a day!

Television can show you just about anything. However, it's you and your family who decide how to use your TV.

How can you see what's happening *right now* on the other side of the world? How do commercials fit between programs? How do they mix real people with cartoons or pictures?

In this book, you'll find out about the science—and the people—that make television what it is. You'll get a first-hand look inside a TV studio. You'll find out how TV signals are sent to homes everywhere. Plus, you'll go behind the **picture tube** (PIK chur TOOB) to find out what makes your TV tick.

Get ready, because we're live and in color!

CHAPTER TWO

TURN IT ON

Remote controls have made channel surfing—switching from show to show—a popular afternoon sport.

One of the first questions most people ask when they sit down to watch TV is, "Where's the remote?" Things are a lot easier now. In the old days people had to get up and touch a button on the TV to do anything. They had to walk to the TV to turn it on, switch channels, or to change the volume. Watching TV used to be a lot of work!

Every television set still has manual controls—buttons—that control your TV. They turn it on and off, switch channels, change the volume and adjust the picture. These buttons are wired to the **circuitry** (SUR kuh tree) in the TV that does all the real work. So how does a remote control do all that, and more, without any wires?

There are lots of different kinds of remotes. Some just control your TV. Others will work with both your TV and VCR (video cassette recorder). There are remote controls for CD (compact disk) players and camcorders (video cameras). There are even universal remote controls that can operate many of these things.

They all have number pads, display buttons, and channel programmers. Some have automatic timers and beepers that go off if you lose them. Basically, they all work in about the same way.

When you push the power button on your remote, it turns on a circuit. That circuit lets electricity flow from the batteries to the *microprocessor.* A microprocessor is a sort of mini computer inside the remote. It looks like a black block with a lot of metal legs that are all wired to a circuit board.

The microprocessor, and other parts of the circuitry, send pulses of electricity to the infrared *light emitting diode,* or LED. An LED is like a mini flashlight bulb at the front of the control.

Infrared pulses from your remote are taken in by your TV's infrared detector and changed back into electrical signals.

WHAT'S INSIDE

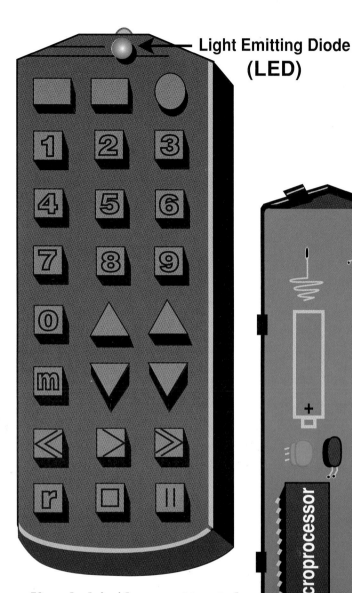

Light Emitting Diode
(LED)

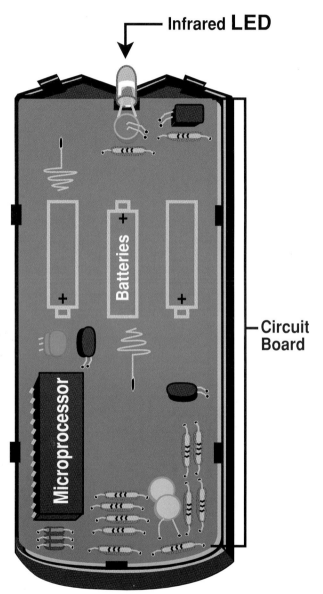

Infrared **LED**

Batteries

Microprocessor

Circuit
Board

If you look inside a remote control you'll see its electronic parts—or circuitry. You'll find batteries, a circuit board, printed circuits (on back of circuit board), a microprocessor, a light emitting diode (LED), and an infrared LED.

Every time you press a button, you're turning on the LED. Then the LED sends an infrared signal to an *infrared detector* in the television set. The infrared detector turns the infrared signal back into electricity. The electric signal tells the TV's circuitry what to do.

Each button you push on the remote has its own special infrared signal. That's so when you push the *channel* changer you won't get surprised and get louder *volume* instead.

Have you ever pushed the button to change the channel and nothing happened? That's because the remote's infrared signal is made up of rays like light rays. Anything that will block light—like a pillow, your feet, or your brother or sister's head—will block the remote's signal. Also, your batteries may need changing.

TV Firsts

1928 The first pictures were transmitted across the Atlantic.

1936 Black-and-white TV service started in London. Color TV didn't begin in the U.S. until 1951.

1937 A company called Dumont built the first TV sets in the U.S. They also experimented with transmitting TV signals.

1939 Franklin D. Roosevelt was the first president to appear on television. He spoke before the camera at the New York World's Fair.

1962 Telstar, a telecommunications satellite, carried transatlantic TV signals.

1967 U.S. Congress created the Public Broadcasting System (PBS).

1969 723 million people watched the first live TV pictures broadcast from the moon.

1976 The Olympics were broadcast around the world for the first time from Montreal, Canada.

1995 The first live TV pictures from the atmosphere of Jupiter were received from Galileo, a satellite made to explore space.

CHAPTER THREE

INSIDE YOUR TV SET

When you turn on your television set, you see **images** (IM ij ez) moving on the screen—people, animals, even cartoons. You also hear sounds that go along with those images—talking, squawking and sometimes music. How does your TV bring things that are happening thousands of miles away back to life in front of your eyes?

PICTURE TUBE

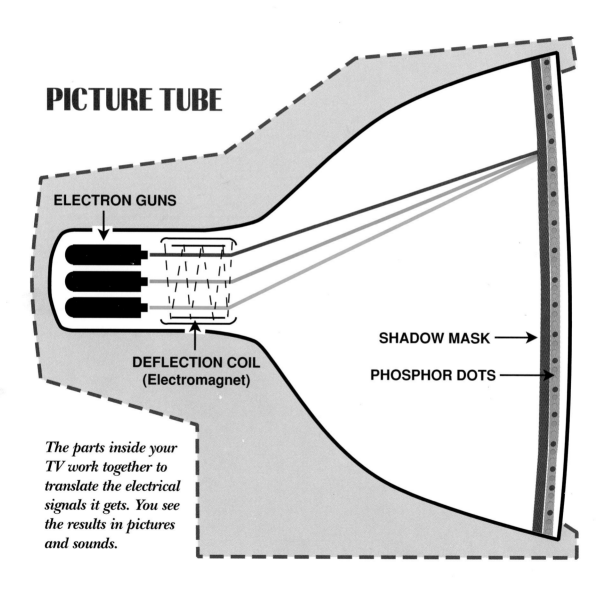

ELECTRON GUNS

DEFLECTION COIL
(Electromagnet)

SHADOW MASK ➝

PHOSPHOR DOTS ➝

The parts inside your TV work together to translate the electrical signals it gets. You see the results in pictures and sounds.

It all starts with an **electrical signal** (ee LEK tri kul SIG nul) that comes into your house. The signal comes through an **antenna** (an TEN uh), a cable or a **satellite dish** (SAT il iit DISH). However the message gets there, your TV translates the signals into cartoons, prime time shows, live **broadcasts** (BRAWD kasts) and commercials, too.

The Parts

Inside a TV, the biggest thing you'll see is the **picture tube.** The screen you watch is part of the picture tube. In back it narrows down into a small circle. Under the picture tube, you'll find a lot of wires, one or more boards with small colored chips wired to them, and a speaker or two. Each gadget you see plays a part in making the sounds and pictures that light up your television.

The boards, wires and small colored chips make up the **circuitry** of the television set. Parts of the circuitry turn the set on and off, and turn the sound up or down. Other parts switch the channels, change color and brightness, and adjust the vertical and horizontal position of the picture.

Making Pictures And Sound

The real work happens when the circuitry picks up and separates the audio (sound) and video (picture) signals sent to your TV. Then, other parts of the circuitry **amplify** (AM pluh fii) these signals.

Your television sends signals for color images to three **electron** (ee LEK tron) guns at the back of the picture tube. Each electron gun "shoots" electrons for one primary color of light. These aren't the primary colors you're used to. Primary colors for light are red, blue and green. Fast as light, the electrons zoom straight toward the screen.

Before they get there, the **deflection coil** (dee FLEK shun KOYL)— a very strong **electromagnet** (ee lek troh MAG nit)—bends the electrons from their straight-shot path to the picture tube. The deflection coil makes the electrons scan over the entire screen, instead of hitting just one spot.

The electrons have one more obstacle before they hit the screen—the **shadow mask** (SHAD oh MASK). The shadow mask is a piece of metal full of tiny holes. These holes make sure that the electrons for each color get where they're supposed to go.

SHADOW MASK

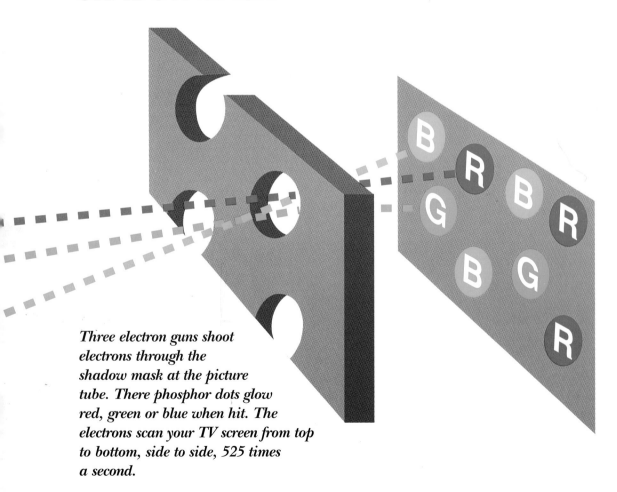

Three electron guns shoot electrons through the shadow mask at the picture tube. There phosphor dots glow red, green or blue when hit. The electrons scan your TV screen from top to bottom, side to side, 525 times a second.

Finally, the electrons reach the front of the picture tube. There they hit one of millions of **phosphor** (FOS fer) dots that cover the screen. When hit with the right electron, a phosphor dot will glow red, blue or green. If no electron hits a phosphor dot, that part of the screen stays black. Blending these colors makes all the other colors we see.

Images on the television don't actually move. They just look like they do. The electron guns quickly scan back and forth, up and down, over the screen. They work so fast that they make new pictures faster than our eyes can follow.

What's a picture without sound? Your TV's circuitry separates the **audio signals** (AW dee oh SIG nulz) from the **video signals** (VID ee oh SIG nulz). Then the audio signal is amplified and fed into the speakers. You control the speakers with the volume button.

Every time you turn on your TV, there's a whole lot of science happening right *behind* the screen. The next time you hear, "Brought to you by ..." you can fill in the rest with "... audio-visual signals, electron guns and phosphor dots!"

Making Pictures Move

The images on your TV screen are made up of millions of red, blue and green dots in hundreds of lines. They all change 30 times a second. These quick changes are faster than your eyes work. So, you see a moving picture.

CHAPTER FOUR

INTO YOUR LIVING ROOM

Do you still have one of those tall, wire TV **antennas** on top of your home? Are you hooked up to cable, or do you have a **satellite dish** of your own? Most people in the United States hook their televisions up to a **cable system** (KAY bul SIS tum). More and more people are buying or renting large or small satellite dishes.

You already know that once the audio and visual signals get to your TV they work the same—no matter how they're transmitted. So why is everybody getting rid of their antennas?

In many places, an antenna just doesn't do the job. Because your local TV stations **broadcast** with a **transmitter** (trans MIT ur) tower instead of a more powerful **satellite** (SAT il iit), your picture might be fuzzy. Your antenna might only be able to pick up two or three local stations.

When you hook up to cable you almost always have a clear picture, no matter how far away the TV station is. Audio and visual signals come to your television through a *coaxial cable* (koh AKS ee ul KAY bul).

A coaxial cable has a central wire that is insulated and surrounded by a second tube of wire. The whole cable is covered with another insulator. With a cable hook-up, you can choose what you want to watch from 30 to 50 stations.

THREE WAYS
TO GET THE SIGNAL

The next step up is a satellite dish. If you live too far away for a cable system to reach you, a satellite hook-up is just what you need. Satellites can also give you more channels to choose from than cable.

A satellite dish is really an antenna, too. It receives **radio waves** (RAY dee oh WAYVZ) from a satellite in space instead of a transmitter on Earth. Satellites that send radio waves orbit the Earth about 22,500 miles out.

A modern communication satellite can weigh several tons (thousands of pounds). It has thousands of parts and is powered by over 15,000 **solar cells** (SOH lur SELZ). The satellite travels in the same speed and direction that the Earth rotates. It's in **geostationary** (jee oh STAY shu nayr ee) or **geosynchronous** (jee oh SIN kruh nus) orbit. That means it stays over the same location all the time. A geostationary satellite over a spot (or place) on the equator stays over that spot because it is moving with the Earth as it turns.

Want To Know More about radio waves? Check out RADIO, another book in the YOU MAKE IT WORK series.

TV satellites get their signals in the form of radio waves from ground stations. The satellites **amplify** the signals and send them back to Earth. Then satellite dishes receive them and turn them into the **electrical signals** our TVs use to make pictures and sound.

TV signals are transmitted to people's homes in three ways. TV antennas pick up radio waves from local TV stations. Cable systems carry their signals through a coaxial cable. Satellites relay radio waves around the world.

A satellite can handle many channels at once, using the power collected from its solar cells. TV satellites make it possible for us to watch programs **broadcast** anywhere the U.S. or around the world.

Satellites also play an important role in cable systems. It's through satellites that cable companies receive the TV signals they send through their cable to you.

Getting Wired

By 1992 more than half of the homes in America—over 55 million—were hooked up to one of 8,700 cable systems. Many countries, and even private companies, had satellites that could handle TV signals in orbit around Earth.

CHAPTER FIVE

GETTING THE PICTURE

Who creates the **images** and sounds we see on TV? Anyone with a video camera and recorder can produce a program for TV. Most TV programs are made in television studios.

A television camera can take your image and turn it into electrical signals.

Changing A Person Into Electrical Signals

Imagine you're the anchorperson for your local news. As you sit behind the desk reading the top news stories, a cameraperson focuses in on you.

Inside the television camera are lenses, mirrors and three **camera tubes** (KAM er uh TOOBZ). Each camera tube is for one of the primary colors of light—red, green and blue. Light reflects off you and goes through the lens of the camera. There it bounces off the mirrors and splits into red, green and blue light.

Interested In Cameras?

Read about camcorders in VIDEO and movie cameras in MOVIES, two more books in the YOU MAKE IT WORK series.

INSIDE A TV CAMERA

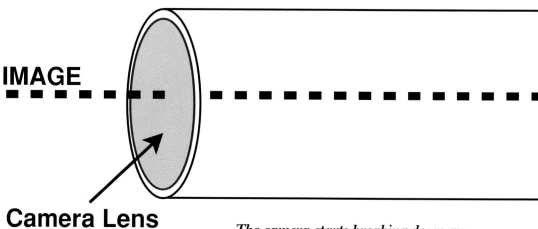

IMAGE

Camera Lens

The camera starts breaking down an image for television by separating light into its three primary colors—red, green and blue.

At the same time, microphones in the studio pick up the sound of your voice. The studio's sound system then turns your voice into **electrical signals** that can be made into radio waves.

When the red light falls on the red camera tube, it makes a red image on a **light sensitive surface** (LIIT SEN suh tiv SUR fis). The same thing happens to the green and blue light. Another part of the camera scans the red, green and blue images and turns them into **electrical currents** (ee LEK tri kul KUR ents). Later, these electrical currents are changed into **radio waves.**

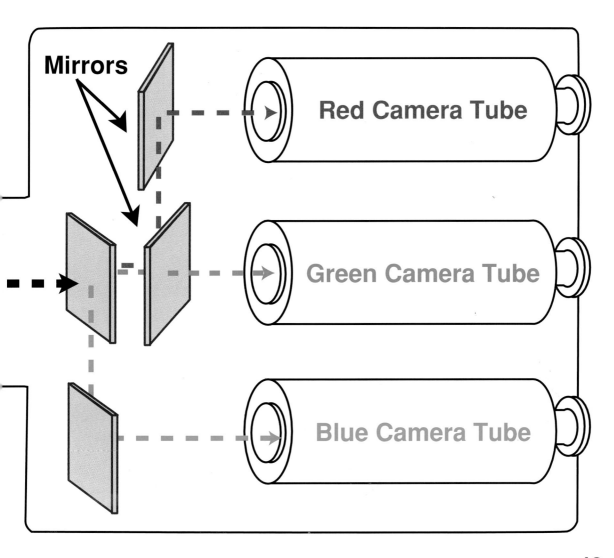

Mirrors

Red Camera Tube

Green Camera Tube

Blue Camera Tube

Antenna towers transmit radio waves that carry video and audio signals from TV stations.

Riding The Radio Wave

Now that your image and voice have been turned into radio waves, the TV station can take the next step. First they amplify your **video** and **audio signals** with their electronic equipment. Then they move your signals to the **transmitter**. From the transmitter they're sent out as radio waves.

CHAPTER SIX

MAKING A TV SHOW

It's time for your favorite show! You sit down, flip on the tube and it starts right on time. You can watch the whole show—with commercials, too—without a glitch. Everything happens just as planned.

This doesn't happen just by chance. Airing a TV show without any mistakes takes time and professional care. Planning and creating a television show is called *production*.

Most programs you watch on TV are **prerecorded** (pree ree KOR did), or made before you watch them. However, the news, sports and weather are usually done live. Everything starts with a *director*, a *storyboard* and a *script*.

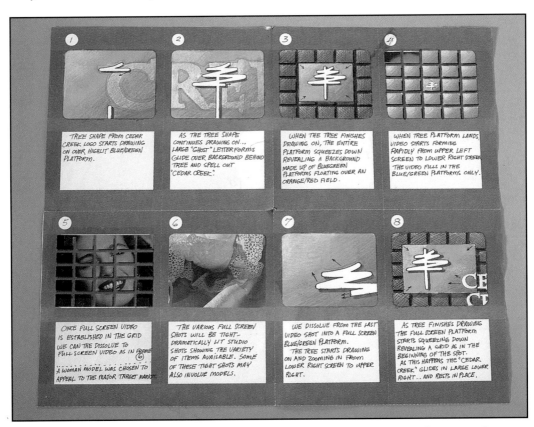

The storyboard is made up of pictures that show, in order, how each scene of a TV program should look.

The director supervises everyone who works on the production. He or she oversees everything that is supposed to happen. Directors get their directions from the storyboard and script. The storyboard is like a giant comic strip. Each picture shows how a scene from the TV show should look.

The script is where all the visual and audio directions are written. They include which camera to use for each shot, whether to do a close-up, add sound effects, and so on. The director, script in hand, sits with the *technical director* in front of the control panel. Together, they plan the production.

The control panel has several monitors, or TV screens. These screens help the director and technical director plan each minute of the program. It's here that any special effects are added to the live action. They can watch one screen to test how it would look to **superimpose** (soo pur im POHZ) pictures, or blend two pictures together.

TV Makes An Impression

When we see something or someone on TV, we tend to form an opinion right away. The first televised presidential debates in 1960 may have helped elect the new president. Some experts say that because John F. Kennedy looked more confident on television than Richard M. Nixon, it helped him win the election.

At the control panel, the director and technical director put all the pieces of a TV show together.

The floor director cooperates with the director and technical director. He or she helps to decide which cameras to use.

The technical director can use still pictures and words to make a complete picture. Also, he or she can ask a *graphic artist* to draw something. Then the technical director uses the control panel to make the drawing exactly the size the producer wants. Words or graphics can fly across the screen, or bounce like a ball.

During all this time, the director and the technical director are also working with the *floor director.* Floor directors help to decide which cameras will be used and where lights will be placed. They also help tie all the parts of the program, plus the commercial breaks, together.

Brought To You By

You might know the names of the people who read your local news. However, you need a lot more people to make the news program happen. On average it takes about 25 to 40 people to broadcast a local news show.

Last, but certainly not least, is the *audio engineer.* Audio engineers operate the audio board. They raise and lower volume levels. They can also bring in music and place the sound so it plays along with the right pictures. Audio engineers use recorded music, sound effects and sounds from other videotapes. They can mix these sounds with the sounds from the studio's microphones. Finally, they record the audio on tape.

Then it's back to the control panel. The technical director ties the video and audio together there. When the director and the technical director are satisfied, they record the program on tape. Then they store it until the time it appears on your TV.

CHAPTER SEVEN

HOW DO THEY DO THAT?

One of the best things about television is that the picture you see isn't real. It's just a picture. You can do just about anything on TV—do an instant replay, change size and shape, mix people with cartoons, even transport from place to place! How do they do that? They're called special effects.

Using the switcher, technical directors change images, add words and create special effects.

The Special Effects Generator

Most of the special effects you see on television are created by the technical director. He or she creates them with a mechanical friend— the **switcher** (SWICH er), or special effects generator. The camera in the studio sends **video signals** to the monitors and to the switcher in the control room. There, the technical director uses the switcher to mix and match pictures.

Using the switcher and the **character generator** (KAYR uhk tor JEN ur ayt ur), the technical directors can call up computer-made letters and characters, or pictures. Then they place them over the **images** from the camera. He or she can also mix in film clips, videos or computer art with the images on the **control room monitors** (kun TROHL ROOM MAHN i turz).

Using special computer programs, the technical director can make pictures do all sorts of tricks. They can rotate, twist, shrink or grow. The computer programs can even take images from two separate screens and push them together on one!

The Value Of Television

The most popular sporting event on TV is the Olympics. In 1968 it cost less than $5 million for TV coverage of the Olympic Games. By 1988, the cost had jumped to over $300 million.

Weather Map Magic

Take a good, close look at the weather forecasters on your local news. Do they ever seem to miss when they're pointing to a thunderstorm, or to your hometown? They have a good excuse. The map you see behind them isn't really there at all!

If you were standing in the TV studio during the news, you would see the weather forecaster pointing to an empty green board. What's going on? One camera is filming the weather forecaster. It sends the image to a monitor in the control room. On another monitor is a weather map.

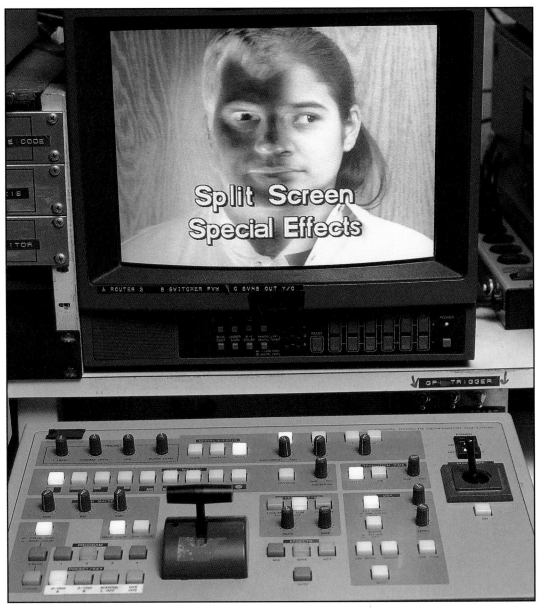

Using a split screen technique, technical directors can make the strangest effects.

Using the switcher, the technical director gets rid of the green board electronically. Then he or she replaces it with the weather map from the other monitor. The two images—the weather forecaster and the weather map—get mixed together so they form one picture. To get their pointing right, the weather forecasters have to watch themselves on monitors set up out of the camera's range.

This effect of replacing a colored background with another picture is called a *chroma key*. The chroma key is a very useful special effects tool. It can mix people with cartoon characters, make people fly, or make a wall seem to burst into flames!

Instant Replay (Instant Replay)

When you're watching any kind of sport, did you ever want to see a play from another angle? Did you ever want to watch the winning score—just one more time? Thanks to instant replay, we can watch the highlights of a game while the game is still being played!

How can that happen? The first thing you need is several cameras covering the game at once. They send their signals to a remote control television production unit. The remote unit is one of those vans with a small dish **antenna** on top. The unit records the camera's signals on tape while the game is being played. When you need an instant replay, they quickly rewind the tape and **broadcast** the recording instead of the camera's live signal.

The Future Of Television – 3-D TV

Right now scientists are working on technology that will bring us 3-D TV. Even better than holograms, you can watch the 3-D images from any angle. You can even walk around and watch the action from behind! Using sound waves to control laser beams, this television will trade in its screen for a cube display. It fits in the palm of your hand.

GLOSSARY

amplify (AM pluh fii) – to increase the strength of a signal, to make it stronger

antenna (an TEN uh) – wire, or other metal object, that transmits (sends out) and receives (picks up) radio waves

audio signal (AW dee oh SIG nul) – the part of the radio wave broadcast by a television station that carries sound information

broadcast (BRAWD kast) – to transmit a television program in the form of radio waves from an antenna

cable system (KAY bul SIS tum) – television sets in the cable system receive television signals by way of a cable instead of an antenna or satellite dish

camera tube (KAM er uh TOOB) – part of a television camera that changes light into electricity

character generator (KAYR uhk tur JEN ur ayt ur) – a computerized machine used to mix letters, characters or clip art with a picture on a control room monitor

circuitry (SUR kuh tree) – all the electrical parts that make up an electrical device, like a television set

control room monitor (kun TROHL ROOM MAHN i tur) – one of several television screens used by the director in the control room to direct the flow of a TV production

deflection coil (dee FLEK shun KOYL) – the part of a television picture tube that uses a strong electromagnet to bend the electron beams and make them scan

electrical current (ee LEK tri kul KUR ent) – flow of electrons along a conductor—like a wire (like **electrical signals**—ee LEK tri kul SIG nulz)

electromagnet (ee lek troh MAG nit) – a magnet that works when electricity is flowing through it

electrons (ee LEK tronz) – negatively-charged particles found outside the nucleus of an atom

geostationary (jee oh STAY shu nayr ee) – an orbit above the Earth's equator that allows a satellite to stay over the same spot on Earth all the time (like **geosynchronous**—jee oh SIN kruh nus)

image (IM ij) – picture

light sensitive surface (LIIT SEN suh tiv SUR fis) – surface that changes when visible light falls on, or hits, it

phosphor (FOS fer) – substance that gives off light when struck by electrons, or other forms of radiation

picture tube (PIK chur TOOB) – part of a television set that changes electricity into images

prerecorded (pree ree KOR did) – something that is recorded before it is broadcast

radio waves (RAY dee oh WAYVZ) – invisible waves that can carry information through the air or empty space at the speed of light

satellite (SAT il iit) – an object that circles the Earth above the atmosphere; it can receive and transmit radio waves carrying television information

satellite dish (SAT il iit DISH) – a circular antenna that can receive radio waves of television programming directly from a satellite

shadow mask (SHAD oh MASK) – a metal plate with thousands of holes in it behind the screen of a picture tube; the holes in the plate direct the electron scanning beam to the right color phosphors on the screen

solar cells (SOH lur SELZ) – objects that can change light from the sun into electricity; they provide electrical power for many satellites

superimpose (soo pur im POHZ) – to place one image over another so that both are seen as a single image

switcher (SWICH er) – a computerized device used by a television director to switch, mix or change images on the monitors in the control room (like a special effects generator)

transmitter (tranz MIT ur) – the place or device that sends out the radio waves that carry the video and audio signals

video signal (VID ee oh SIG nul) – the part of the radio wave broadcast by a television station that carries picture information

INDEX